MW01027133

THE GATHERING OF MY NAME

Books by Cornelius Eady:

Kartunes
Victims of the Latest Dance Craze
Boom Boom Boom
The Gathering of My Name

THE GATHERING OF MY NAME

poems by
Cornelius Eady

Carnegie Mellon University Press
Pittsburgh 1991

GOSHEN COLLEGE LIBRARY
GOSHEN, INDIANA

ACKNOWLEDGMENTS

Some of these poems have appeared, at times in different versions, in the following publications: *Contact II, Crazyhorse, Harper's, Obsidian II, Pequod, Ploughshares, Seneca Review, The William and Mary Review* and BOOM BOOM BOOM (State Street Press Chapbook Series, 1988).

The author would also like to thank The Writers Room, NYC, an organization which receives partial funding from the National Endowment for the Arts, for workspace from 1988 to 1990.

Publication of this book is supported by grants from the National Endowment for the Arts in Washington, D.C., a Federal agency, and from the Pennsylvania Council on the Arts.

Cover art: *In E Sharp* by Romare Bearden, courtesy of ACA Galleries

Library of Congress Catalog Card Number: 90-84781
ISBN 0-88748-115-9
ISBN 0-88748-116-7 Pbk.
Copyright © 1991 Cornelius Eady
All rights reserved
Printed and bound in the United States of America
First Edition

TABLE OF CONTENTS

V

This book is for
June Jordan and David Sheehan

Gracias.

I

GRATITUDE

I'm here
        to tell you
                an old story.
                This
Appears to be
        my work.
                I live
                in the world,
Walk
    the streets
                of New York,
                this
Dear city.
        I want
                to tell you
                I'm 36
Years old,
        I have lived
                in and against
                my blood.
I want to tell you
                I am grateful,
                        because,
                        (after all),
I am a black,
        American poet!
                I'm 36,
                and no one
Has to tell me
        about luck.
                I mean:
                after a reading
Someone asked me
                once:
                    If
                you weren't

Doing this,
          what
                    (if anything)
                    would you be doing?
And I didn't say
                    what we both
                              understood.
                              I'm
A black, American male.
                    I own
                              this particular story
                              on this particular street
At this particular moment.
                    This appears
                              to be
                              my work.
I'm 36 years old,
                    and all I have to do
                              is repeat
                              what I notice
Over
     and over,
               all I have to do
               is remember.
And to the famous poet
                    who thinks
                              literature holds
                              no small musics:
Love.
     And to the publishers
                    who believe
                    in their marrow
There's no profit
               on the fringes:
                    Love.
                    And to those

Who need
        the promise of wind,
                    the sound of branches
                    stirring
Beneath the line:
            here's
                another environment
                poised
To open.
        Everyone reminds me
                    what an amazing
                    Odyssey
I'm undertaking,
            as well they should.
                        After all,
                        I'm a black,
American poet,
            and my greatest weakness
                        is an inability
                        to sustain rage.
Who knows
        what'll happen next?
                    This appears to be one
                    for the books,
If you
    train your ears
            for what's
            unstated
Beneath the congratulations(!)
                    That silence
                        is my story,
                        the pure celebration
(And shock)
        of my face
            defying
            its gravity,

So to speak.
        I claim
                this tiny glee
                not just
For myself,
        but for my parents,
                        who shook their heads.
                        I'm older now
Than my father was
                when he had me,
                        which is no big deal,
                        except
I have personal knowledge
                of the wind
                        that tilts the head back.
                        And I claim
This loose-seed-in-the-air glee
                on behalf of the
                social studies teacher
I had in the tenth grade,
                a real bastard
                        who took me aside
                        after class
The afternoon
        he heard I was leaving
                        for a private school,
                        just to let me know
He expected me
        to drown out there,
                        that I held the knowledge
                        of the drowned man,
The regret
        of ruined flesh
                in my eyes;
                which was fair enough,

Except
    I believe I've been teaching
          far longer now
          than he had that day,
And I know
    the blessing
        of a
        narrow escape.
And I claim
    this rooster-pull-down-morning glee
            on behalf of anyone
            who saw me coming.
And said yes,
      even
        when I was loud, cocky,
        insecure,
Even
    when all they could have seen
          was the promise of a germ,
          even
When it meant
    yielding ground.
        I am a bit older
        than they were
When I walked
    into that room,
        or class
        or party,
And I understand the value
    of the unstated push.
        A lucky man
        gets to sing
his name.
    I have survived
        long enough
        to tell a bit

Of an old story.
            And to those
                        who defend poetry
                        against all foreign tongues:
Love.
        And to those who believe
                        a dropped clause
                        signifies encroachment:
Love.
        And to the bullies who need
                        the musty air of
                        the clubhouse
All to themselves:
                    I am a brick in a house
                                that is being built
                                around your house.
I'm 36 years old,
            a black, American poet.
                                Nearly all the things
                                that weren't supposed to occur
Have happened, (anyway),
                and I have
                        a natural inability
                        to sustain rage,
Despite
        the evidence.
                    I have proof,
                    and a job that comes
As simple to me
            as breathing.

II

GRACE

Perhaps
It's the deep, endless
Whirr of the expressway
In the background I need to
Keep, the shadows

At this time in the afternoon,
Their fingers and blouses
Across the lawns and steps.
Perhaps it's these kids,
Negotiating games in the street,

The sight of a blue car
Parked in front of a
Blue house.
              After a week of rain,

The sun is out, a neighbor
Waxes her black sedan.
From my window I watch
The neighborhood compress
And shimmer on the hood,
A simple trick
              of the light.

NOTHING

I have often wondered how it really felt,
And now it silts my hands.
What am I doing?
What if I told you the truth:
Tracing my arms through the air,
Watching snow fall outside the window.
How would you feel if I told you
This was how I spent my time?

I roll it on my tongue.
I play its tension like a rubber band.
I polish its dull grey coat with oil.
Is it sickening how I wait for it to
        curl about my legs?
And the watering of my eyes
        as it calls,
And the apparent stiffening
        of my limbs.

What can I say?
You see how it is.
You see how it fills me.
You see how I shake from its roar.

Eddie Son House's Death Letter Blues

I got a letter this mornin'
How you reckon it read?

He's not quite himself tonight,
Partly because of alcohol, partly
Because of what he'd be in this suburban home
Without a guitar and slide
On his lap.

There are nine hard lacquer sides of him
Somewhere in his prime, a voice
So hair-raising not even the two-bit
Fly-by-night engineer could do it harm.
The folk society found the right person,

But his hands are inarticulate.
The first thing he does, without playing
A note, is to give everybody

The hard stuff: *Friends,*
Mumbles his scrunched back,
Let me tell you about leaving.
Then you notice his scooped face, feel
The old man's mask shift its weight
Beneath your cheeks, hear his voice, realize
That there is a button of ruin in the throat,

That any accident might set it off one night,
Start it, and leave it running. Embarrassed,
Embarrassment blues, life-song of a man
You won't catch spooling onto
The tape.

Though he's not the same and not getting paid (again),
Eddie's game: he bow-wows into the mike
I hope you never get them, children,

But.

NOBODY'S BUSINESS

You have cheated me
    and I still love you.

You have lied
    and I still love you.

And the neighbors tell me you're nothing but
                nothing but
                nothing but

    and I still love you.

Love is dope
Love is dope
Love is dope

And my degrees
    wither to paper.

And my smart wardrobe
    slips out of context.

You walk over me
    and I still love you.

You mock me to your friends
    and I still love you.

I have tasted your hand
    and my brother can't tell me
    and my mother can't tell me
    and my father can't tell me
    and my sister can't tell me
    and the college can't tell me
    and the talk show host can't tell me
    and Jesus
            Jesus coming to warn me in my sleep
    can't tell me

What the hell
        what the hell

I guess there's
        a police blotter in my future

What the hell
        what the hell

I suppose I'll be
        a mystery corpse

What the hell
        what the hell

The easy smile
        has its way

        baby
            baby
        baby
            baby
        baby
            baby
        baby

                baby
                    baby
                baby
                    baby
                baby
                    baby
                baby

        candy
            candy
        candy
            candy

            candy
                        candy
            candy

            What the hell
                        what the hell

I guess I'm grown, now
                        what the hell

I guess I'll nurse
                        this bruise

            DON'T LIKE IT?

THE SUPREMES

We were born to be gray. We went to school,
Sat in rows, ate white bread,
Looked at the floor a lot. In the back
Of our small heads

A long scream. We did what we could,
And all we could do was
Turn on each other. How the fat kids suffered!
Not even being jolly could save them.

And then there were the anal retentives,
The terrified brown-noses, the desperately
Athletic or popular. This, of course,
Was training. At home

Our parents shook their heads and waited.
We learned of the industrial revolution,
The sectioning of the clock into pie slices.
We drank cokes and twiddled our thumbs. In the
Back of our minds

A long scream. We snapped butts in the showers,
Froze out shy girls on the dance floor,
Pin-pointed flaws like radar.
Slowly we understood: this was to be the world.

We were born insurance salesman and secretaries,
Housewives and short order cooks,
Stock room boys and repairmen,
And it wouldn't be a bad life, they promised,
In a tone of voice that would force some of us
To reach in self-defense for wigs,
Lipstick,

Sequins.

YOUNG ELVIS

He's driving a truck, and we know
What he knows: His sweat
And hips move the wrong product.
In Memphis, behind a thick
Pane of glass, a stranger daydreams

Of a voice as tough as a Negro's,
But not a Negro's. A voice that
Slaps instead of *twangs*,
But not a Negro's. When it
Struts through the door
(Like he knows it will), and
Opens up, rides

The spiky strings of
The guitar, pushes
The bass line below the belt,
Reveals the drums
As cheap pimps,
In fact transforms the whole proceedings
Into a cat house, a lost night . . .

He wets his lips.
Already the young driver is imagining
A 20th century birthday present,
The one-shot lark of his recorded voice,
The awe he intends to
Shine through his mother's favorite hymns.

CAR ALARM

It's a cheap or discontinued model, the kind
That won't cycle shut until its
Owner returns, red-faced,
One hopes, ears clobbered
By various suggestions.
Isn't it funny, my wife asks,
The way we adapt to
Intrusion, and yes, I have
To think, even as she says this,

That I have never been forced
To hear Beethoven,
Whose first symphony plays
Over our clock radio,
In quite this manner, have
Never considered the sound
Of a world, nagging against
Its interpretation.

It's a new way
To translate the noise
As we wait, and the bedroom
Fills with the morning's first insults.

LEADBELLY

You can actually hear it in his voice:
Sometimes the only way to discuss it
Is to grip a guitar as if it were
Somebody's throat
And pluck. If there were

A ship off of this planet,
An ark where the blues could show
Its other face,

A street where you could walk,
Just walk without dogged air at
Your heels, at your back, don't
You think he'd choose it?
Meanwhile, here's the tune:
Bad luck, empty pockets,
Trouble walking your way
With his tin ear.

WILLIAM CARLOS WILLIAMS

Didn't like jazz, he once claimed
In an interview,
The good doctor's reaction to it
A bit like a hand retracting
From a slim volume

Of 20th century verse. In
Other words: good intentions,
But what does this *yak, yak, yak*

Have to do with me? This,
You understand, from a person
Who had listened
To an industrial river, forced
A painter's brush to give up
Its low, animal noise,

Broke trees into
Sense.

INSOMNIA

You'll never sleep tonight.
Trains will betray you, cars confess
Their destinations,

Whether you like it
Or not.

They want more
Than to be in
Your dreams.

They want to tell you
A story.

They yammer all night and then
The birds take over,
Jeering as only
The well-rested can.

FUN

for Michael Collier

You wish to sleep, to close your window to the singing,
But you can't it's so sweet;
The whoops, the hard blues piano
Tumbling drunk and forgetful
    out of the barn door.

So you listen to what the revelers wish to state:
We need *baby, baby, babies*
(The rest of the lyrics are mumbled),
And we can be better than the person
    who stood earlier
At the cocktail party, dying
With a drink in his hands.

That wasn't really us floats through the window.
Here we are: listen.
And the piano barks,
The voices tighten and yap,
Tickling the night with *what the hell.*

                Breadloaf, August 1986

Alabama, c. 1963: A Ballad by John Coltrane

But
Shouldn't this state have a song?
Long, gliding figures of my breath
Of breath
Lost?

Somebody can't sing
Because somebody's gone.
Somebody can't sing
Because somebody's gone.

Shouldn't this landscape
Hold a true anthem?

     What
You can't do?
     Whom
You can't invent?
     Where
You can't stay?
     Why
You won't keep it?

But
Shouldn't this state
Have a song?

And shall we call it
My face will murder me?
And shall we call it

I'm not waiting?

SONG

Nigger-Lover is a song, spat out
Of an open car window
At dusk,

At the great mall in
Lynchburg, VA, the
First time in

Five years we've
Heard it. We
Almost made it,

Amazed this hasn't
Happened before. It
Was the end of

Our going away party.
We were walking out
Across the lot. What

Those drunken boys in
The black Chevy saw
Was so obvious. What

Else could they make
Of this invitation?
We almost made it,

Always carried the possibility
With us for years.
But it was

The end of our
Going away party. Almost,
Almost, almost got out

Scott-free, almost
Didn't have
To hear it

Right where
You are supposed
To hear it, almost

Didn't have to drive home
Thinking hard about
The headlights

At our backs, carry
Their hard singing
Away in our

Cars, in our heads. We
Almost, almost,
Almost

Got away. We were just
Walking out, soft
Twilight

In the hills surrounding
The lot, laughing
Our plump laughs,

Nearly gone.

THELONIUS MONK

I know what to do with math.
Listen to this. It's
Arithmetic, a soundtrack. The motion

Frozen in these lampposts, it
Can be sung. I can lift away
Its logic, make it spin

Like an orbital satellite, find
Gambling's true pitch.
It can be *played*:

Adventure, the trying of
Patience, holding back, holding
Up, laying out, stop-time,

Slow motion, time travel,
Space walking. It can be
Splintered, strained

Through the fine mesh
Of a second. Now I try
A few bars of *what's next?* Run

It over my hands, ignite it,
Make the fire sound like
April in Paris.

MUDDY WATERS & THE CHICAGO BLUES

Good news from the windy city: Thomas Edison's
Time on the planet has been validated. The guitars
And harps begin their slow translation
Of the street, an S.O.S. of what you need
And what you have. The way this life
Tries to roar you down, you have to fight

Fire with fire: the amplified power
Of a hip rotating in an upstairs flat
Vs. the old indignities; the static
Heat of *nothing, nowhere,*

No how against this conversation
Of fingers and tongues, this
Rent party above the
Slaughter-house.

THE SOLOS, SARAH LAWRENCE COLLEGE

A sparrow, chirping itself silly
Somewhere beyond my field of vision,
Catches my ears, such a little deal
In the courtyard. Silence,
Silence, silence and then
A sweet burst of notes and
What was I thinking of? The wind
Hits the leaves, and there's
A high green sizzle in the air.
Then (God's truth!) a saxophonist
Opens up; first a recording
Of some favorite player, then
I hear a rehearsal of a blues,
The questions one asks
When no one is listening.

HANK MOBLEY'S

Sorry, Hank.
Found out
The Hard
Way. Back
Of an
Album cover,
Years later,
Browsing in a
Record store. It's
The wrong way
To find out.
The guy who
Wrote the
Notes on
The liner
Was pissed.
It appears
That a lot
Of papers
Decided not
To run an
Obit since
By then you
Were not
Quite
John Coltrane.
So this poem
Could be about
The breaks,
And this poem
Might be about
Fire, or
The lack
Of it,
Or this poem
Could deal
With the also-rans,
—You know,

The joke
About the
Guy who
Invents
1 through 6 Up
Then quits,
Throws up his hands
In desperation,
But it was
Your breath
In my ears
As I stood there,
Dumbly speaking
To whom?

III

THE GRIN

I saw it
On the mouth of a
Plainclothes cop
At the Norfolk airport.
Running from the gate
To the taxi stand made me his
Business.

A black man, bolting
For an exit, is a
Sweet suspicion.
"Will you cooperate?"
He asked. It wasn't
A question.

That was the first time. When
It happened again, same
Circumstances, same face,
I realized the grin on it,
Barely held in check,

Was his trademark.
He let me go.
"See you soon,"
He said
       to all of us.

SHERBET

The problem here is that
This isn't pretty, the
Sort of thing which

Can easily be dealt with
With words. After
All it's

A horror story to sit,
A black man with
A white wife in

The middle of a hot
Sunday afternoon at
The Jefferson Hotel in

Richmond, VA, and wait
Like a criminal for service
From a young white waitress

Who has decided that
This looks like something
She doesn't want

To be a part of. What poetry
Could describe the
perfect angle of

This woman's back as
She walks, just so,
Mapping the room off

Like the end of a
Border dispute, which
Metaphor could turn

The room more perfectly
Into a group of
Islands? And when

The manager finally
Arrives, what language
Do I use

To translate the nervous
Eye motions, the yawning
Afternoon silence, the

Prayer beneath
His simple inquiries,
The sherbet which

He then brings to the table personally,
Just to be certain
The doubt

Stays on our side
Of the fence? What do
We call the rich,

Sweet taste of
Frozen oranges in
This context? What do

We call a weight that
Doesn't fingerprint,
Won't shift

And can't explode?

GOSHEN COLLEGE LIBRARY
GOSHEN, INDIANA

The Wrong Street

If you could shuck your skin and watch
The action from a safe vantage point,
You might find a weird beauty in this,
An egoless moment, but for
These young white men at your back.
Your dilemma is how to stay away from
That three to five second shot
On the evening news of the place
Where you stumble, or they catch
Their second wind, or you run up
To the fence, discover that
You are not breeze, or light,
Or a dream that might argue
Itself through the links. Your responsibility
Is not to fall bankrupt, a
Chalk-marked silhouette faintly
Replaying its amazement to
The folks tuning in, fist to
Back, bullet to mid-section.
Your car breaks down
And gives you up. A friend's
Lazy directions miss
The restaurant by two
Important blocks. All of this
Happened. None of this
Happened. Part of this
Happened. (You dream it
After an ordinary day.) Something
Different happened, but now
You run in an
Old story, now you learn
Your name.

FALSE ARREST

What seemed to have bothered him the most, after it was done
And he began to re-create his story for the T.V. reporter
In front of the same park bench where he had first seen
The pair of cops that would, when he approached them
To ask directions, look him over and see

What? grab him and cuff him and whisk him to
A hospital, dope him and then let him go
The next morning, innocent, what seemed
To have broken him was the second
He realized something had

Gone wrong or too far, and all that would be left
Was the right to see the moment fall,
Taking him with it, mouth agape perhaps,
The way a trout, caught, swallows that first,
Painful cup of air,

A taut desire pulling its jaw toward
What it never dreamed it
Could taste. The cops scuffle and
Tug him towards their
Squad car, a small crowd
Gathers and hoots

And suddenly he looks dead
At the camcorder, the
Moment becomes private, as if
We were sitting with him
In a doctor's office, surrounded
By the blossoms of his
Small complaints, things

He should have paid attention
To sooner than this, a professional
But disinterested prognosis
Cutting him away.

SPIC

for Cathy

This time, all they do
Is roll the window down,
Framing your body
After they pull the car
Over the lip of the curb.

This time, it only goes this far.
No bullets, no spit,
No hard clack of a door
Announcing its desire
To spring open.

This time, you're let off with just a reminder.
There are cat calls, a loose
Slice of male tongues, a dumb
Prayer of turf.

They mis-pronounce your complexion, black woman,
And roll away, you think,
For darker skin.

Why Do So Few Blacks Study Creative Writing?

Always the same, sweet hurt,
The understanding that settles in the eyes
Sooner or later, at the end of class,
In the silence cooling in the room.
Sooner or later it comes to this,

You stand face to face with your
Younger face and you have to answer
A student, a young woman this time,

And you're alone in the classroom
Or in your office, a day or so later,
And she has to know, if all music
Begins equal, why this poem of hers
Needed a passport, a glossary,

A disclaimer. *It was as if I were . . .*
What? Talking for the first time?
Giving yourself up? Away?
There are worlds, and there are worlds,
She reminds you. She needs to know
What's wrong with me? and you want

To crowbar or spade her hurt
To the air. You want photosynthesis
To break it down to an organic language.
You want to shake *I hear you*
Into her ear, armor her life

With permission. Really, what
Can I say? That if she chooses
To remain here the term
Neighborhood will always have
A foreign stress, that there
Will always be the moment

The small, hard details
Of your life will be made
To circle their wagons?

IV

JUNE 14TH, 1988

Three governesses in the park
With their tiny charges
From the other world. O, the
Boredom in those
Great hips! as the women
Steamboat their carriages,
One, two, three across the
Path. They are a slow wall,
Dream-drudging their way

Beneath the full
Branches, a muted poster
Of wives.

THE MOUSE

The unexpected appearance of a mouse
In the cafeteria of the Museum of Modern Art
Briefly indexes my memory to a picture in
The *Encyclopaedia Britannica* of a
Kangaroo rat, my naive, elementary schoolboy
Belief of good vs. bad
Pests. It is that cute, and moves

With such indifference my ears begin to tune themselves
For the sound of a child or mother
Pet hunting, a jangle
Of blush and small
Misgivings. It's slightly larger
Than my thumb, harmless
In its desires, but since it's
Confirmed, for once, my peripheral
Vision, I rise from the table

As if I were about to give it
My evolutionary seat, one species
Admitting its shortcomings
To the Next Big Thing. How
Do we deal with it, this
Kinetic ambassador that
Has suspended forks and conversations,
Brought us all eye-to-eye,
Finally.

THRIFT

What happens when an old black man,
Toothless and raggedy,
Walks into a bank, catches
Some young, white, middle-manager's ear
With a slurred tale of coins
Hoarded from his wife and kids
(Who would only have spent them),
Leftovers from various hits
On the numbers, plus
God knows how many
Easy deceptions.

If you were this man, what
Would you do with this true believer
Who has walked through the 'door
Of your bank, fired up
With what he has pulled off,
Knowing that on some non-verbal level
He has encoded you
(Or someone like you)

As kindred, that only you
(Or someone like you)
Could understand this type
Of fidelity. And somehow
He guides you to the door
And through the glass you see
The trunk of this man's car,
My father's car, its springs
Low and ripe as the apricots
Sweetening on his tree
At home. He wants to give you

The weight he has built, penny
By penny. He wants you to lift
Away what you first thought of him,
Bag by precious bag. And he wants
You to do it, now.

PASTORAL

There is the car, which won't start.
It's busted, and furthermore
The damn thing's *whirring* in the middle

Of the street, and the poor sucker driver
Is pissed off. He's in the middle
Of the street,

The street is in Manhattan, and so
You have to consider what the guy
In the white

Caddie behind him might have
Under his coat, and you hope
The poor, red-faced S.O.B.'s

Luck won't run from bad
To worse, hope he doesn't
Leap from behind his wheel

Sopping wet with embarrassment
And scratch the other guy's
Finish. That's

The sort of story
The *Post* loves to fish
From the police blotter, the

Type of incident
You were warned about
In driving school. *Never*

Never never say
A damn thing
Until the police

Arrive, my instructor
Told me, and meanwhile
A crowd has gathered, a

56

Line of cars
Idle like butter
In a fat man's vein.

Dental Hygiene

The dentist looks
At my broken mouth
The way I'd look

At a child who
Innocently yells
The word "Nigger"

Then smiles, a baby Jesus.
Is there an alibi
For this? That's

What I hear beneath
Those weekly sighs.
Poverty? Child abuse?

Look at this, he sighs,
And gives me
The yiddish word

For *dirt,* and I
Understand, by
His tone, that a person

Who carries this word
Between his teeth
Chooses to live

Somewhere beyond kinship.
Look at this, he sighs,
Exposing the residue

Of a ton of meals
To the light, hard
Yellow diamonds

Of what I like,
Of what I have swallowed,
Will swallow again.

He *tut-tuts* again in yiddish,
As he scrapes, and I
See myself dressed

In sackcloth,
Singing this poem
As I stumble barefoot

Through the marketplace,
Rattling my fool, black
Teeth out.

ATOMIC PRAYER

If the bomb drops
And I'm riding the
Staten Island Ferry,
Give me time to spit in the water.
If the bomb drops
And I'm on top
Of the Empire State Building,
Give me time
To toss a penny
Off the observation deck.
If the bomb drops
And I'm approaching the subway,
Let me have the chance
To jump the turnstile.
If the bomb drops
And I'm walking down Fifth Ave.,
Grant me a loose brick,
A fresh plate glass window.
Grant us a moment
When there'll be no need
To play it safe.
Give to us the pleasure
Of misdemeanors.
Let each of us do
What we've always
Dreamed of,
But were too polite
To act out.
Let us extract
Our brief revenge,
Spilling and ripping things
We've been taught
Not to handle.
If we're to die before we sleep,
Grant us a moment to uncover
The secrets behind the door marked RESTRICTED,

Authorize us to touch what was always held
                just beyond our reach.
Give us a taste
Of the stolen world.

LIVING WITH GENIUS

It's sundown, and we
Find Gertrude Stein sitting
In her parlor at the
Piano. She's about
To give Alice B. Toklas
The night off. Gertrude
Wants to see if
A piano
Can imitate a violet. Gertrude
Wants to be alone
When she does this, suspecting
That what she wants to do

Is insane. The sun
Sets and Alice
Starts to worry
About her boss; what is
This shit about violets,
Violets, violets,
Anyway? Gertrude
Demands a glass of whiskey,
The shades drawn and all
The lights turned off. With
Pleasure, you old
Coot, Alice thinks
To herself. She does
As she's told and
Goes to bed.

Gertrude
Sits in the dark
All night.

In the morning
She starts thinking
About roses.

WHITE SOCKS

It is important to remember
That there is a place
For everything.

Those white socks,
For example,

They were important
Maybe twenty years ago,
But now
They are
An embarrassment.

This is not meant
To insult you.
Some of my best friends
Have no taste.

Nor am I afraid
To be seen with you:
As you must know by now,
I was born
Without fear.

But listen to reason.
You know
We can't go
Anywhere
With you wearing
White socks.

Let's talk it over.
Let's clean out your dresser
And then
Walk shoulder to shoulder
Into the future.

WEST 3RD STREET, THE FIRST WEEKEND IN JUNE

Across the street, a neighbor
Carefully dusts his shoes off.
Leaning out his window,
He places one inspected pair
On the fire escape, slowly
Begins on the other, his ragged
Yellow wash towel working
At it, no polish here, just

A critique of wear, a lifting
Of dust from scuffmarks. He hauls
The shoes in, shakes the towel
Out, his head tortoises home,
And he is rid of something.

ROMARE BEARDEN RETROSPECTIVE AT THE BROOKLYN MUSEUM

Opera! All that cardboard
And newsprint roars, a chorus:
Sweat, Jazz and Jesus,
Big women lifting their skirts,

A hot breeze down 125th Street,
Subways demonstrating the snake dance,
Cigars, bop and the numbers,
The infra-red tenements
(Cigarette lighters of the Gods),

Murder, pig meat, and let's not forget
The vertigo which powers the trumpets,
The lightning the drummers twirl above their heads,
The concealed weapons and still-born patents.

Here's the nervous tic of a culture we thought
We checked at the door,
The headlines of a world
That threatens to rip open.

Intermission on East 7th Street

He says:
Save my life, buddy,
Save my life, buddy,
Save my life, buddy.

I just got out
          of the hospital
I just got out
          of the hospital
They just let me out
          of the hospital

              hey

It's February in New York
and you can see I've got
          no money,

You can tell by my style
I carry
          no visible means,
and it's February in New York.

              hey

It's cold and I don't wanna work
(you know what they expect for small change?)
It's snowing, it's cold

But it must be hot for you,
You and those fine ladies
          you're walking with.

              hey

Save my life, buddy.
I ain't no actor doing this for a poster.
You know what I am

This city know what
        I am. I
                just got out
                just got out

A little bread'll change it.
I want money—
                —who doesn't?
But I ain't a crook.

I'm sick of it
        —I want a hold on my life

I'm sick of it
        —I want a hold on my life

I'm sick of it
        —I want a hold on my life.

The View from the Roof, Waverly Place

By accident, I gaze at
These two young guys
Standing on the roof across
From my office window, a moment
Otherwise theirs. They watch
And listen to Sixth Avenue.
They talk. They have time
In their lives for a smoke.
Then the one on the left loops
His arm around the other's shoulder,
—My *buddy*, *my buddy*. They have
A quilt of lives spread below them,
The cool thrill of looking down.

BLUE MONDAY

And as my commuter train
Rolls through morning Harlem,
My eyes catch a young black woman,
A squatter vs. the neighborhood
And the shell of the building
That surrounds her, white helmet
Of a bandanna as her arms
Reach and swing a half moon clean
On the outside window. This woman

Is an announcement, world:
Savanna grasses breaking
The scorched earth.

v

THE SHEETS OF SOUND
for Xam

I

He says:
What do I have to lose,
                    Actually,
By coming right out
And saying
          What I mean
                      To say?
Like this,
          And like this,
And like this
Breathing
          Rickety steps
To the heart
Of the matter? Loose
                    A black spirit
Around the joint?
Mr. Coltrane, floating
     a l i n e
Like this, pushing
     its muscle,
                hell,
Discovering its sweet
     worth:
The sweet worth
               Of pushing
Any damn wall.
This is
        A necessary
                    Lesson: You
Can make an art
Out of sailing
               Right over
                         The top, spin
A heart clean,

If only for
       These brief seconds,
              Close the world,
Its silly wounds
And hard manners
        With a yell.
             I hear you push it,
A quote,
A necessary lesson.
        There are gifts,
Aren't there? You ask:
          What do I have to lose
If I come right out
And test it? Peel back
        The romance
In a breath? As you reach
For what?
      Surely this love,
I hear you sing,
This
  Sort
Of
  Love
Will ruin me.
      A wonder operates here.
              Pushes away
The damn wall
As you leap,
       Dresses the shadows
          In the corners
Of the room, speaks
For you,
    Breezes
       Up your throat,
Opens.
How many times
      Can you do this?
         Push
Your losses

74

Open?
      Map the blues'
                Currents?
I hear
    What if
Color the air
        With the danger
Of asking.

II

A man
    Who gives himself
          A right to speak,
A fine spray
Of what he knows,
      Of where he's been,
             What has
Happened to him.
An axe
    Which cuts,
        Impatient,
A loud humility,
A spiritual
     Science,
       Hear it?
In the skirt of the fine, African-American mother?
       Hear it?
In the squeezed life of the black civil servant?
Ask the Harlequin,
      Or the man with the jackal's face,
            Ask the schoolgirl,
Sharpening a mental knife,
Or the King of the margins,
      With the strength of nations
          etched by
          minimum wages,

Or little Johnny Volcano,
Spacing in and out
        Of whatever world'll have him,
                Or long, tall cool,
Who sparks up
Only after
        He folds away his chauffeur's uniform,
                The dark scholar,
Obscured by his teeth,
Diminished
        Each time he laughs
            A fine spray
Of what goes on
Who gets swallowed
        Who takes it
            Who jumps,
A concentration
Of who gives in
        Who shakes it off
            A fine spray
Of what it might sound like
If they could open their lives.

If they could blow it out.

III

        I hear proof,
                survival take a verse,
        I hear proof,
                survival take a verse,
        I hear proof,
                survival take a verse,
        I hear proof
            claim, swing,
        Associate itself,
                I hear proof

Declare, the outer layers
                    slough off,
I hear proof's beat, its wide fingers
          roll seconds on its tips,
I hear proof's laugh, a deep glide
          from the stomach's pit:

          T h i s   i s   w h o   I   a m ,   a n d
          T h i s   i s   w h o   I   a m ,   a n d
          T h i s
          I s   w h o   I   a m .   I   h e a r

Proof's river, the deep bass spring
          which feeds it,
The trance of keyboard light
          upon water,
I hear proof's memory, a torch of calf skins
          lighting a cave;

          T h i s   i s   w h o   I   a m ,
          A n d   t h i s   i s   w h o   I   a m ,   a n d
          T h i s
          I s   w h o   I   a m .   I   h e a r

Proof gather the sweet/sour berries of its name.
I hear proof,
          survival take a verse,
I hear proof,
          survival take a verse,
I hear proof,
          survival take a verse.

IV

          I try to imagine that first attempt
               on the bandstand,
          Try to figure how that first breath

                              grew wild,
              Troubled the curve of the
                              mouthpiece,
              Chance's sweet flavor as he
                              leaned towards the microphone.
              What would you do if a man
                              fell to the ground
              And in that moment, decided
                              that this act was song,
              Decided, as he fell, not to
                              mind the falling, to
              Name it something else. Think of it:
                              both of you
              Locked in that first, grand inarticulate slur.
                              What to say to a man
              Who is shredding decorum, blowing it
                              across the club
              In streamers? Imagine this spectacle
                              as it shakes down, the slant
              Of those first notes,
                              the announcement

              As it bumbles against a cocked ear.

V

              I heard a story, once,
              Told on Miles Davis and
              The young pup, John
              Coltrane,
              Who was seeking out
              The master's
              Wisdom, sort of
              Sitting at his feet,
              So to speak,
              And he asked Mr. Davis
              To reveal to him

The secret of how
To finish
A solo,
And Miles sort of
Grunts like a
Baptist mother,
And he tells
Coltrane:

"Take the
Damn horn out
Of your mouth"

VI

He has discovered
The only way

To pose the question,
The only language

That might fit
The equation.

This will
Be his:

This yearning
To tell all,

The balm against
A soul's distraction.

He knows
                this
Can be the only canvas

Supple enough
                    to take it,

After years
Of exploring

The café standards
At the gigs, in

The studios,
Beautifying

Each and every
Possible nuance.
                            This
Is his only way out:
To decode

What nags
At his breath,

To have his tongue
Own the name
                    Of what it chases.

VII

I am driving
            With a friend
                        In New Jersey:
Two poets discussing
Jazz
        In a moving vehicle!
                        When the conversation
Somehow floats over to

Coltrane,
                And for the first time
                                Our talk develops holes.
The long and the short of it:
You confuse him, John.
                                C'mon: Is the world really
                                                Like *that* at the core
All the time?
The fee for the search
                                So high?
                                He's referring, of course,
To those moments
When the only thing
                Between you and dissolving,
                                                The only thing
That can win you back
Is McCoy,
                Hemming you in a
                                Loose blouse of notes.
What about this,
My friend wants to know,
                                What
                                        Do you call it—
—Jazz?
It's the spin he puts
                On the word
                                That sinks
Everything.

VIII

        "A Love Supreme"

                        BUT
                        How long
                        Can you listen

To bullets
Hitting
Sanctified tin?

You can believe
What it must cost him,
These thin sheets of
Hard translation

A bk tongue
Is a coiled danger

Is trouble[2]
trouble. A bk tongue

Is a trick mirror,
Lightning

And the fuse
And this

Beauty
Is a danger is
A sound called

When the
Water breaks
Called what if

After
Murder

After
Terror

After
Servitude

After
Disappearance

After
Displacement

After
Short change

After
Guff, the child's portion,
The revised story

The wake-up call
Got through
Anyway?

IX

I tune my ears to my name.
I dream
          what I carry,
I taste
          what can't
Be swallowed,
I shake to
          what I cry.
I come from
          a long line:
My mother
          canned fruit,
My sister
          used her beauty,
My niece
          inherited my impatience
My brother
          never found his mind.

How do I sing them?
We are not sweet:
                    these are lives
One walks around, yet
                        locked in the throat
The angels of our Gods, claimed and unclaimed

                                                    choirs.

How
To admit their song
Against the world,
                    against the facts,
The acquired urge to gaze down?

X

Once, I listened to you
                Recreate
                        The world.
It was one
Of your later gigs.
                You made
                        A few statements.
I heard it
        Only once,
                    Years ago,
And I still remember
The way the horns
                Blew primeval
                            Slop,
Which cricketed into
Gills,
        Wings,
                Fur,
Roared until a new language
Decided itself, reared
                    On its cool, black limbs.
                                        You were close
To being spent.

84

I heard it
       Only once,
              An outrage stretched over
Two sides
Of a four-sided record.
              I remember the way the cymbals
                           Spat the weather
out,
Seas percussed
Against the piano's
       Terra firma.
             I have carried this
For years;
How we tumble with it,
        How we can never
Get it all out.

Carnegie Mellon Poetry

1982
The Granary, Kim R. Stafford
Calling the Dead, C.G. Hanzlicek
Dreams Before Sleep, T. Alan Broughton
Sorting It Out, Anne S. Perlman
Love Is Not a Consolation; It Is a Light, Primus St. John

1983
The Going Under of the Evening Land, Mekeel McBride
Museum, Rita Dove
Air and Salt, Eve Shelnutt
Nightseasons, Peter Cooley

1984
Falling from Stardom, Jonathan Holden
Miracle Mile, Ed Ochester
Girlfriends and Wives, Robert Wallace
Earthly Purposes, Jay Meek
Not Dancing, Stephen Dunn
The Man in the Middle, Gregory Djanikian
A Heart Out of This World, David James
All You Have in Common, Dara Wier

1985
Smoke from the Fires, Michael Dennis Browne
Full of Lust and Good Usage, Stephen Dunn (2nd edition)
Far and Away, Mark Jarman
Anniversary of the Air, Michael Waters
To the House Ghost, Paula Rankin
Midwinter Transport, Anne Bromley

1986
Seals in the Inner Harbor, Brendan Galvin
Thomas and Beulah, Rita Dove
Further Adventures With You, C.D. Wright
Fifteen to Infinity, Ruth Fainlight
False Statements, Jim Hall
When There Are No Secrets, C.G. Hanzlicek

GOSHEN COLLEGE - GOOD LIBRARY

3 9310 01045061 5

PS
3555
.A35
G3
1991

DATE DUE

1987
Some Ga
Other Ch
Internal C
The Van
A Circus
Ruined Ci
Places and

1988
Preparing
Red Letter
The Aband
The Book
Changing t
Weaving th

1989
Recital in a
A Walled C
The Age of
Land That
Stations, Jay
The Comm
The Burden
Falling Deep
Entry in an

HIGHSMITH 45230

1990
Why the Rive
Staying Up For Love, Leslie Adrienne Miller
Dreamer, Primus St. John
Two Long Poems, Gerald Stern

1991
Permanent Change, John Skoyles
Clackamas, Gary Gildner
Tall Stranger, Gillian Conoley
The Gathering of My Name, Cornelius Eady
A Dog in the Lifeboat, Joyce Peseroff
Raised Underground, Renate Wood
Divorce: A Romance, Paula Rankin